MW01232319

DAY TRADING WITH OPTIONS:

The Newest Guide to Apply the Most Effective Day Trading Strategies at the Options Market to Generate a Consistent Monthly income

ROBERT MURPHY

Introduction

Day trading is a career that you have to invest time into. If you have decided to try it out, you have to spend time in practicing it before you start live trading. As you practice, you improve your strategies. Only then, do you use live money to try it out? All these need you to invest your time. Day trading isn't something that can be done successfully only when you have the urge for it. You must spend your time and energy into it if you want to succeed.

If you have decided that trading is something that you want to consider, you should think of starting up as little as possible. Go for few stocks or currencies initially, instead of trying to enter the market with a boom, and at the end of the day, you thin yourself out. If you go all out initially, you will end up confusing yourself, and this could lead to a large number of losses.

It is advisable that you are calm while you trade. Shut off your emotions while you purchase. Use only facts and don't try to make use of emotions because they could mislead you.

The more you are able to take out the emotional aspect, the more you can be faithful to the plan that you have laid out. When you are calm, it permits you to be focused.

Day Trading vs. Swing Trading

When it comes to the world of trading, people have different thoughts, meaning that different schools of thought exist on what should be done. A highly debated topic is if short-term trading such as in the form of day trading or trading long term such as in the case of position trading should be opted for.

The traders in both schools feel that their styles are better than the other. They go ahead to think that theirs make more money compared to the rest. We will analyze the facts and come bearing the truth. If you try out day trading, will you become more precious than a position trader or vice versa?

Should you dash in and out of different markets, imitating a sprinter? Should you stay in a market longer than the sprinter in the case of a marathon runner?

We will look at what is available before we conclude.

Day Trading

Before we state which, one is better, let's talk about their differences. What day trading means is the opening, as well as the closing of positions on a particular day.

One perk of day trading is that you aren't allowed to hold a position past a day. This means you don't have to disturb your head about how a trade is faring while you slumber.

You quickly know where you fall into once the day ends. You can quickly tell if you have lost or earned a profit.

One disadvantage of day trading is the fact that daily you have to seek for a new trade. This could be stressful for some, but easy for others.

Swing Trading

This is another type of trading, where a trader tries to catch the swings in changes of price in a bid to capture a significant amount of the brand-new movement.

To execute this, you need more experience and strategies. These will allow you to know the way a perspective movement would occur.

Swing traders are known to analyze their charts daily in a bid to find that opportunity which could lead to a significant movement in a few days to come.

Immediately such an opportunity is spotted, they have it traded in and try to manage it for a few days.

A perk of swing trading is the fact that there is no need to be in a position daily before money can be made. The right trade could earn you a great reward to risk ratio. This means that if everything goes as planned, you can make a pile of money from that single trading decision. The issue is whether this would everything go as planned. Novices should avoid this in the game of trading.

It involves experience to predict what would happen after a thorough analysis has been made.

A significant disadvantage is a fact that it involves a large amount of predicting the price. This means that it resembles art and not science. Apart from that, you have no choice but to watch as your profits and loss on that trade you made a move down and up within a period. This isn't meant for the weak-hearted or those scared of losing.

Buying Long, Selling Short

It is time to look at some of the different strategies that you can use to make day trading successful for you. By this time, you may have already used a few different approaches and tried out day trading a little bit. We are going to start out with one of the intermediate strategies that you can use to see some great results. And we are going to start with the selling short strategy.

Selling short is going to be the sale of some kind of security or another financial instrument a seller has borrowed in order to make a quick sale. The seller thinks that the security they adopted is going to decline in price, which means that it will be easier to purchase that security at a lower price later. The difference between what the security was sold short at, and the amount that it was purchased at, is going to be either the loss or profit for the seller, depending on the numbers you have.

Anyone is able to short any instrument or any asset, including stocks, bonds, currencies, commodities, and hybrid securities. Any company that has some shares that they will trade on the market will usually have millions of shares that their stockholders will hold onto. These stockholders may include individual and institutional investors, employees, managers, and executives. However, all these people are going to have a common interest, and that is how they want the company to continue to succeed in the future. This is the way that they earn money on the stocks. The result of this is going to be that the shares appreciate over time and provides wealth to the shareholders.

Anyone is able to purchase the shares of a company as long as they have money to invest in it. Investing in stocks has long been a popular means of accumulating wealth. Many times, an investor is going to purchase shares of different companies and they will either trade them off quickly or hold onto them for a more extended period of time. Buying shares are known as going long, and long is only going to refer to investors that buy stocks and don't short them. For example, mutual funds would be going long without any short stocks.

These kinds of stocks are easily bought with cash or through another account known as a margin account. If the investor is able to pay some money, they will pay off the total amount that the stock is worth. If they are working with the margin account, they will spend part of the amount before borrowing the rest from their broker, using the stock as their collateral. You would do short selling with a margin account if needed.

Investors are often going to go long when they have the hopes of seeing an increase in the price of the stocks. Traders will then go short when they hope the cost of the capital will tumble. When they sell quick, this allows them to sell a stock that they don't technically own. The reason that they can do this is that they borrow the stock from the brokers and then they will sell that stock at the current price of the market. The profits will then be credited to the margin account of the seller. And if they earn enough in profit, then they get to keep the rest. Then, in the future, the seller will be able to cover their short position by purchasing it and repaying the stock that was loaned back to the broker.

The difference that comes up between the sale and the purchase price will end up being the loss or the profit for the seller based on how much they were able to benefit from the sale.

This idea of short selling is often a topic that is much misunderstood in investing. Short sellers are often seen as callous individuals who will try to get a gain no matter what it costs. They are regarded as people who don't care that much about the companies or individuals who may be destroyed in this process. However, the truth about these kinds of traders is quite a bit different. You will find that short sellers, when they are successful, will allow the market to function better because they will add more liquidity to the mix, and they will restrain any over-exuberance that occurs with the investors in the market.

Too much of this optimism can drive the stock market to really lofty levels when it is a peak time. The process of short selling is going to be a reality check that will keep the stocks from being raised to extraordinary heights during these times. Shorting is risky because it is geared to go against the trends in the market. And you will find that it can get more perilous as the market starts to surge. This is why it is often reserved for traders who have some experience with the market and know more about what they are doing.

The idea and the process of short selling is something that most traders are not familiar with. Many people are used to doing the average buy low, sell high when they invest. There are very few who know about the sell high and buy low. When you do short selling, it will allow you to profit from stocks that tend to drop in price. Basically, you are going to borrow shares from your broker to sell, and then you return those later on. If you are lucky and can read the market well and your trade works well, you can then purchase those shares at a lower price than what you sold them at.

Retail vs. Institutional Traders

In the world of trading, there are basically two forms of traders: institutional and retail. The difference between them dictates the way they approach their trades. For example, institutional traders usually make large trades as compared to retail traders. But what are they exactly?

Their names might just give you a clue as to what you can understand about them.

Retail traders refers to individual traders. These traders can be anyone in the world who has the ability to get in on a trade. On the other hand, institutional traders are those who represent large financial institutions, hedge funds, banks, or other big firms that manage money. You could say that institutional traders are "corporate" traders whereas retail traders are "home" traders.

1. What's the Day Trading with Options

When trading straight calls and puts, one of the best ways to earn profits is through day trading. Although options are not stocks, the same day trading rules apply to trading options as they do with stocks. This means that you have to know what the definitions are of a day trade and what the legal requirements and risks are.

Day trading options can be both desirable and lucrative because small price movements in stock, which happen all the time, are magnified in options. You can use day trading to get into options when prices are relatively low, and then you can get out when they reach a pricing level that represents an acceptable profit level for you in the same day before prices begin moving in the other direction again.

The fact that a $1 move in a stock price can represent a $10 to $100 move in an options price is what makes this approach very attractive. However, understanding how options are treated is essential, as well. If you are unable to meet the requirements to day trade options, you can still do it a few times a week, as we will discuss in a moment.

Options Tickers

Remember that each option has its own ticker. This is important because day trading involves day trades of the same financial security. In other words, if you buy and sell Apple stock on the same trading day, that is a day trade. When it comes to options, however, buying and selling two different options on Apple stock does not constitute a day trade. To understand why, note that an opportunity is defined on the underlying stock, in addition to the predetermined factors (strike and expiration). It also depends on the type of option. To continue our example above, a call option set at $240, with a deadline of 12/12/2019, is not the same financial security as a call option set at $240, with a period of 12/30/2019.

In the same breath, a call option with a strike price of $240 and an expiration date of 12/12/19 is not the same financial security as a put option expiring on 12/12/2019 with a predetermined $240 strike price.

So, the first thing to keep straight in your mind if you want to day trade options are what is the same financial security for the purposes of day trading and what is not.

Day Trading: Defined

A day trade involves buying a stock or option and then selling that same stock or option before the close of the same trading day. Anyone is allowed to do a limited number of day trades, but what brokers and regulators are looking for is what is known as a pattern day trader. A pattern day trader, by definition, is someone that makes 4 or more day trades in any five day period. A five-day period means five consecutive trading days, so a weekend does not reset the counter. These days, most brokers will track the number of day trades you have in your account for you. So if you are looking to make some day trades but don't want to be labeled as a pattern day trader, you can make up to three day trades, and then wait for the counter to drop to 2 or below.

Day Trader Requirements

Federal regulators consider day trading to be a high-risk activity. So, while it is legal, there are rules in place designed to keep day traders from causing brokers too much financial trouble should their trades go badly. The primary state that you have to be aware of is that a day trader must have $25,000 deposited in their account. You also have to open a margin account. This is a large sum of money to put up for many people so that they might be effectively cut off from day trading. But if you are able to open a margin account and deposit the required sum, then you are free to enter into as many day trades as you like. Of course, we hope that you won't be running out of the $25,000 if you choose this path but becoming a day trader on an official basis will open up a lot more opportunities for you. Stocks are continually moving up or down by small amounts, with trends that last a few hours or throughout the day that will end up generating substantial changes in options prices. Getting rid of the day trade limitation not only lets you trade frequently, which will give you take advantage of more of these trends when you can spot them, but it will also allow you to make high-volume trades. If you are subject to the day trading limitation, meaning that you do not have a margin account with $25,000 in value in the report, you may get notices about day trading limitations if you try to trade multiple options in a single trade.

In other words, if you try trading 10 Apple options, all with the same strike price and expiration date, you might be told that you will not be allowed to sell all ten choices on the same trading day. If you become an official day trader, then these types of restrictions would be lifted, giving you a lot more flexibility when trading.

Day Trading…Without Becoming a Day Trader

If you are unable to deposit $25,000 in a margin account or simply want to avoid becoming a pattern day trader, you can still use day trading as a part of a broader options trading strategy. In this case, you might want to trade options in a way that utilizes three or fewer day trades in every five trading day period. This can allow you to make three lucrative day trades per week that can help to boost your overall trading revenues. The only issue with this type of trading activity is the fact that you must avoid making too many day trades over a given five-business day period. If you are careful about preventing this problem, then this is not going to be an issue for you.

You can also effectively day trade by letting your businesses run overnight. Technically speaking, this makes you a so-called "swing trader." A swing trader holds their positions overnight, for a few days, or even weeks. In practice, any options trader is a swing trader because all options contracts expire. So, in reality, there isn't any other way to be when trading options, except a day or swing trader.

If you are really looking to day trade but want to avoid adding to your day trade account, there are two ways to go about doing it. The first way is to start in the morning looking for trends to trade on. Then you enter your trade and hold it overnight, provided that the profit you are going to make is going to account for the losses that could occur from theta or time decay. So, if you've earned $100 during the day and theta is -0.12, you know that your profit is going to be automatically reduced by $12, but you might be willing to accept that small decline in profits. You can wait for the markets to close and then enter an after-hours sale order, which will be executed at the market open. Or you can wait until the market opens before actually placing your order.

Alternatively, you can enter your positions just before market close, if you suspect a trend is going to carry through the following day. You will do this knowing that you are going to take a hit on the price of the option at the market open due to the theta or time decay.

This procedure can be very tricking, of course. The reason is that a lot of action can happen at the market open, and this can wipe out your positions if it is not something that works in your favor. For this reason, day traders of stocks don't hold opinions overnight. But the risk with some options contracts is going to be lower than it would be trading a highly volatile penny stock the way that day traders of stocks do.

Max Loss and Take Profit Values

Trading with the trend is a risky activity, and you should always set specific conditions that you use to exit your trades. This is going to involve defining the maximum loss that you are willing to take. Do this on a per option basis per trade. For example, you might decide you are ready to make a $50 loss on a business. That means you are willing to let the price of the option drop $50, and if it doesn't reverse course, you will sell to cut your losses at $50. This is per option contract, so if you are trading 20 options on a trade, the total loss would be $50 x 20 = $1,000.

Why do this? One of the mistakes that beginning options traders make is they will see losses mounting as a stock ends up going in a direction that is the opposite of the trend the trader was aiming for, but they will sit around hoping that the trend is going to change course and go their way. Many traders are willing to do this while watching their money vanish before their very eyes. It's better to get out earlier and cut your losses. It's true that sometimes, you will have gotten out too soon and missed an opportunity when conditions did the reverse, and the option could have become profitable. But on average, when losses reach a certain point, that is basically the end of it. As a trader, you need to be focusing on typical behavior and accept the fact that, sometimes, your decisions are going to result in missed opportunities.

Likewise, a smart trader uses profit values in their trading. For example, you might have a rule that says you are going to sell your options contracts when they reach $50 per contract. Of course, you are going to miss some cases where the stock price keeps moving up or down in the right direction to support more increases in the values of the options that you end up selling early. So, there are going to be missed opportunities for profit. But those missed opportunities are going to pale in comparison to the total losses that are you more likely to suffer when greed takes over the mindset of a trader.

What happens, more often than not, is that traders get giddy when they are watching options prices increase. Then they hold on, hoping to earn more and more money. But options prices can switch gears and move very fast, so they might find themselves in a losing position or at least sitting at a location with fewer profits than they could have had if only they'd applied a take profits rule.

Then they hold on, many hoping to, at least, get back to the previous level of profits that they could have taken but failed to do so. But instead of the benefits coming again, the options keep losing money, and eventually—often, very quickly—the trader finds that they are in a losing position.

The only way to avoid these kinds of problems is to follow set rules, and this is more important if you are going to be using day trading as a strategy. That's because things move really fast in the options world, especially if you are going to be putting yourself in a position where you are buying and selling on the same day. But this rule actually applies to all options traders. You need to play on the averages, not necessarily looking for one big trade. If you are looking for one big business to save the day, eventually, you are going to be looking for a huge win that isn't even possible.

2. How Can I Use Day Trading for Options

When day trading, you shouldn't be concerned with a company's fundamentals, e.g., earnings, industry statistics, or industry position. You shouldn't even be involved with the products or services they're providing or who their Board's Chairperson is! All you have to concern yourself with is the stock's price movements or action, technical indicators, and stock price chart patterns. It's the same if you day trade other market-driven securities.

Managing Trades and Position Sizes

The way you manage or handle your day trades can spell the difference between more frequent winning trades than losing ones. Most newbie traders make the mistake of just passively waiting for their stocks or securities to hit either their profit-taking or stop-loss levels. And this is why they continue to remain newbies.

The pros, on the other hand, know and accept the reality that passively waiting for stocks or securities to hit price targets isn't sufficient to consistently make winning trades. Why? Through experience, they know that when taking positions in specific stocks or securities, traders have limited information on how the market will subsequently behave and how valid their assumptions are about the stocks they took jobs in. And the prices of the commodities will continue to move after taking open positions in them. As the stock prices move subsequently, they'll validate or disprove the assumptions traders have when they took open positions.

Trading the Flag

Here are the steps to implement this day trading strategy:

When one of your SIPs has reached a new significant high for the day, wait for its price to drop or correct after reaching its new significant top for that day.

While observing and waiting for it to establish its support level, decide your position size, and your stop-loss and two profit-taking levels.

If it establishes a support level at a higher price than its low for the day, then take your initial long position in that stock or security close to that support level. To manage your situation well, do not make a full position; just in case, it drops even closer to the support level (remember cost averaging?).

For this strategy, use the support level as your stop-loss trigger, i.e., if the price drops further and below this support level, liquidate your positions to limit your losses. By averaging down, you will also reduce your potential losses.

If the stock's price rebounds, liquidate half of your position at your first profit-taking level. At this point, you can adjust your stop-loss limit upward to your buying price.

If it hits the second profit-taking price, liquidate your remaining positions. If it falls down to the buying price level, liquidate the remaining shares so you can lock in on your first trading profit.

Trading the Low-Float Flag

This trading strategy's ideal for stocks below $10 and with low float, i.e., less than 10 million shares circulating in the market. A caveat to this strategy: your trading platform must be really fast to execute it timely. Here's how to implement this strategy:

When one of your SIPs' prices are surging, wait for its price to start consolidating or stabilize. Don't jump in right away to chase this SIP.

While observing the stock or security's price during consolidation, establish your position size, and stop-loss and profit-taking levels. Ideally, set your stop-loss trigger at the support level of the consolidation band and your first profit-taking trigger at the resistance level of the same group.

When its price starts to approach the upper band or limit of the consolidation stage, take your first long position, e.g., 50% or 70% of your intended position size, depending on how confident you are of your assumptions about the stock. If it falls after you buy but doesn't reach the support level, buy some more to average down.

When the price hits your profit-taking level, sell half of your position and adjust your stop-loss trigger upward to your buying cost or average buying cost level, in case you averaged down earlier.

When the price hits your second profit-taking level or your adjusted-stop loss level, liquidate everything.

Trading the Reversal Patterns

Remember, everything that flies has to land and everything that crashes will eventually fly again. That's just how stock prices are. That being said, there are several reasons why stocks start to sell-off rapidly.

The first reason is the big institutional traders/investors have begun unloading their positions and have started to dump them to the general investing public, resulting in tanking of the stocks.

The second reason can be short selling of the stock as traders hear of some potentially disturbing news that can send a stock's price crashing. However, short sellers will need to cover their positions later on, which mean there will be a surge of buying pressure on the stock that'll push it back up soon.

The window where short sellers start covering their short positions will be the open door for entering a particular stock or security. This window is also referred to as a "short squeeze" because it causes a quick price reversal.

There are four crucial components to any trading strategy on reversals. These are:

In a 5-minute chart, there's a minimum of five upward or downward moving candlesticks.

The stock will either have one of two extreme relative strength indicator (RSI) scores: above 90 or below 10. The RSI is a statistical measure that compares the strength of recent gains versus recent losses and ranges from 0 to 100. An RSI of above 90 means a stock or security's already overbought, buying pressure's already losing steam, and its price is already due for a downward reversal. An RSI of less than 10 means a stock or security's already oversold, selling pressure's already losing steam, and its price is already due for an upward reversal. Se

Set your scanners to identify which of your SIPs are already overbought or oversold via RSI to time your positions, whether long or short.

The stock or security is being traded near the day's established resistance (for top reversals) or support levels (for bottom reversals).

Indecision candles, i.e., spinning tops or Dojis, appear to signal a potential trend reversal. This is your cue to stand by and get ready for a potential day trade, when trading reversal patterns, one of the most telling signs of a possible trend reversal are indecision candlesticks, i.e., Dojis. Indecision candlesticks indicate that an increasing number of the governing party, buyers or sellers, have already started to think twice and have started to stay on the sidelines, hence the indecision.

Recall, too, that Dojis are candlesticks with bodies shorter than its wicks or tails. A bearish Doji, also called a shooting star, is characterized by a long cord and short tail and indicates four essential things:

The opening price for the previous period, indicated by the upper line of the body;

The closing price for the previous period, indicated by the lower line of the body;

The highest price for the previous period, indicated by the top of the wick; and

The lowest price for the previous period, indicated by the bottom of the tail.

Having a much longer wick than a tail, the shooting star tells you that at some point during that period, the bulls were unable to sustain the highest price and the bears overpowered them for the most part, keeping the opening and closing prices close the lowest price. It indicates more substantial selling pressure than buying pressure, which may signal a possible reversal of a bullish period.

Having a much longer tail than wick, the hammer tells you that at some point during the period, the bears were unable to keep the price down and the bulls overpowered them enough to keep the opening and closing prices much closer to the period's highest price. This indicates more substantial buying pressure than selling pressure for the period and may be signaling a possible reversal of a bearish trend.

When trading reversal patterns, use Doji candlesticks to spot stocks whose trends may soon reverse and that may offer potentially profitable day trading opportunities. Reversal pattern-based strategies require clear confirmations of trend reversals or a trend reversal that may already be starting.

The worst thing that can happen is being caught on the wrong side of trading a reversal pattern, which many traders also refer to as catching a falling knife. What this means when it comes to trading reversals is you don't want to take positions on the assumption that the trend will reverse soon. If the prices of stocks are dropping, don't take long positions yet but instead, wait for a confirmation that the lost has already ceased and has already reversed. If the prices of stocks are soaring, don't short sell on the assumption that it will quickly reverse its bullish trend but instead, wait for a confirmation that the bullish trend has already ended and changed.

Three critical indicators to watch out for that may give you the highest probability that a trend has already reversed or is already reversing are:

An indecision or Doji candlestick;

The first candlestick 1 or 5-minute candlestick to reach a new intra-day high (for bottom reversals) in a series of consecutive candles with new lows or a new intraday low (for top setbacks) in a series of successive candles with new highs; and

A relative strength index or RSI of above 90 (overbought) or below 10 (oversold).

When you see both of these, take long positions at prices near the day's healthy support levels (bottom reversal trading) or take short positions near the day's most potent resistance levels (top reversal trading). Your post taking points must be at the first relevant 1 or 5-minute candlestick and near the critical support or resistance levels.

For long positions on bottom reversals, your stop-loss trigger should be the lowest price for the day. But if the price suddenly consolidates after your entry, it may be a sign that it's strengthening before resuming its bearish trend, which means it's better to get out than stay longer. Your profit-taking triggers can be a moving average (an EMA or VWAP) or a specific intraday price level of your choice.

For short positions on top reversals, your stop-loss trigger should be the opposite, i.e., the highest price for the trading day. If the price suddenly shoots back up after a significant drop, it may be consolidating before resuming its upward trend, which isn't what you're hoping for. In this case, it's better to err on the side of caution and close your position by covering your short situation a.s.a.p. On the other hand, your profit-taking triggers can be an EMA or VWAP, or a specific intraday low price levels.

Your key to identifying stocks for day trading using reversals is the following:

Your SIPs with RSIs of either less than 10 or higher than 90;

With significantly higher than usual trading volume, which rises towards the price action's direction and peaks at the reversal point; and Five consecutive increasing or decreasing candlesticks capped by an indecision candlestick or Doji.

3. The Simple Step You Need to Start Day Trading With Options

Jumping into the market may seem like a big deal, and you may be uncertain of the right steps that will make this happen. Some of the steps that are needed to start your day trading journey will include:

Pick out the capital

When you are ready to enter into your trade, you will need to have a set amount of capital willing to invest. You could trade on the margin, which is where the broker will lend you some money so you can make more significant trades, but this is incredibly risky in day trading, and as a beginner, it is not recommended for you to do this at all. The best bet, to ensure that you are going to make smart trading decisions, without increasing your risks, is to just use your own money for each trade.

Before you start trading, and while you are researching, consider setting up a savings account and adding a little money to it each month. Then use this money for your trades. This way, you know exactly how much you must spend, and you aren't guessing or trying to come up with money that you don't have later when your trade doesn't turn out the way that you want it.

Your broker will require that you add the money to the account when you are ready to start trading, so make sure it is prepared to go. You can also add some extra to the account to begin so that it is prepared to go any time that you see a potentially good trade that you want to get in on. Once you earn some profits, you can then withdraw them into another account of your choice.

Choose a broker

One of the most important decisions you are going to make when you first get started with day trading is picking out a broker. This will determine the types of securities you can trade (for example, many brokers aren't going to work with cryptocurrencies for trading), how much you pay for each of your trades, and what kind of platform you get to use. Picking out a reputable broker, someone who is easy to work with can make a big difference in the results you can get with your trades.

The biggest thing to consider when you work with a broker, after determining that they do trade in the securities you are interested in, is their compensation plan. You want to check this out to see if it is going to be beneficial to you and your trading method. Since day trading requires a lot of small transactions during the day, you don't want to end with a compensation plan where the broker gets a set fee every time you execute a trade.

There are a lot of different fee structures that your broker can choose, and you need to learn and agree to the one that makes the most sense to you. Going with a set fee for the whole year would be ideal, but you can also work it out that you pay a percentage of your earnings, so if you don't earn anything on a trade, you won't be missing out. No matter which broker you decide to go with though, make sure to discuss the fee structure with them from the very beginning.

Learn about the market

As you are getting set up with your broker, take this time to start reviewing the charts and the information that are present about your chosen security. As a beginner, it is probably best to pick maybe a handful of guards to work with. And don't work with all of them on the same day. Have a rotation, so if one security isn't doing well on a particular day, you can check out the others and use them for investing instead.

You need to learn as much about the market for that security as possible. Pull out charts on that particular security, looking at how it has done today and on a daily basis, over the past few weeks, and even over a few months or a few years. While day trading only takes place within one day, it is still a good idea to look at more extensive ranges to get a good idea of how the stock has performed in the past, and how it is likely to achieve in the future.

We will take some time to explore more about these analyses, but you may find that working with fundamental analysis and a technical analysis at this time can really help you make smart decisions with investing. First is the technical analysis. This is basically what we already talked about where you will spend time looking over the charts, the history of how the security has performed, and information about the market, and then base your investment decision on that information.

Another option you can use when learning about the market is known as a fundamental analysis. With this method, you are going to look a bit further than the numbers on the page. You will look at who runs the company, what products the company sells, how long the company has been in business, the amount of debt to income they have, and more. To some investors, knowing these things makes it easier for them to decide whether or not they want to invest in a company.

Take advantage of all the tools that you can get your hands on. Use the charts, find some reputable news organizations, and then if your broker is able to provide some additional materials, make sure that you use these too. While you won't want to spend months looking over the charts because then you will miss some great trades (and the market is continually changing anyway to spending too much time can leave you behind), getting a good overall understanding of your chosen securities can make trading easier.

Experiment a little

In some cases, your broker may be willing to give you a trial run on the platform that they use. If you are given this opportunity, then take it. This not only helps you to get familiar with the platform and see if you like it, but it also allows you to do a few sample trades and know how you would fair if you were using real money. You could execute a few businesses and figure out what you need to work on, maybe see if one or two strategies work for you, and more.

Now, not all brokers are going to offer this kind of service to their customers. If it isn't provided, there are still chances for you to play with the market and see what will happen. You can pick a stock or two that you would be interested in, and then pretend that you invested. Follow the share, using the strategy that you choose and then see how the trade would go.

This can help you in a few ways. First, it gives you the chance to watch the market and try out a few trades, before you have to put your actual money into the investment. Yes, you may miss out on some good deals that may have made you some profit. But this is a time for learning, and it can protect you from some bad trades as you get more familiar with the market.

Once you have had a chance to do a few trades, you can then enter the market. You have a bit of experience behind you and maybe even more caution with the businesses because you know that, after the experiment, a few of your trades wouldn't have gone as well as you had thought.

Decide your entry and exit points

When you enter into the stock market, especially with day trading, you must have a strategy from the very beginning. If you just go in with the idea that you want to make money (which is a given because who wants to go into day trading or any other type of trading and lose money?), and nothing else planned out, you are going to end up losing a ton of money very quickly.

Having a plan to enter the market makes things work out well because you will begin at the time that provides you with the highest potential for profits. Many people like to look at the moving averages of the security and then when they see that the security gets under this point, they will enter the market. This allows you to get the guard for a discount compared to normal, and increases your chances of earning any profit, while also increase how much potential profit you can make.

While picking an entry point may make sense, many people wonder why they need to spend their time coming up with an exit strategy as well. Shouldn't you stay in the market as long as possible and get as much as you can? The problem here is that the exchange with day trading is going to be very versatile and there will be a lot of ups and downs that come with it. If you aren't careful about it, and you don't make a plan, you may end up losing more money than gaining.

If you were able to enter into the market below the moving average, then your exit point should be either when the security reaches the moving average, or slightly above this point. Only set the exit strategy above this point if you have plenty of evidence to prove that it will get there. Then, as soon as the market moves up to that point, you can end the trade and enjoy the benefits of your profits.

It is also a good idea to set an exit strategy in case your trades don't go the way that you want. While everyone hopes that they do good business and see profits, even the best traders are going to run into troubles sometimes. The market doesn't always react the way that we would like, and it may go down, even when the signs were all pointing up. Without a good exit strategy in place, it is easy to make mistakes with the trading and then stay in the market too long, resulting in a lot of lost profits. Set a small exit point on this one so that if you do lose money, at least it is only a little bit. Overall, if you are careful with your trading, hopefully you won't have to use this. But it can really help to protect your investment, and you can always re-enter the market later if you find it steadies out then in the day.

Getting started in day trading options doesn't have to be a difficult task. There are a lot of people who like to get started with day trading, and they have high hopes that they will be able to see a lot of profits with the work that they put in. If they are able to get started with the right steps, and really know how day trading works, then they will be able to get started and see amazing results.

4. How to Find Good Options to Trade

If you want to execute a profitable day trade, it all begins and ends with choosing the "right" securities for day trading. Many newbie day traders give up easily because of mostly losing trades, not knowing that the primary reason for their losing trades is the inability to choose their securities well. Don't make the same mistake.

If you choose securities whose prices are as animated as a person on valium or whose trading volume is as high as that of a small private corporation operating in the Himalayan mountains, forget about profitable day trading. When it comes to day trading, it behooves you to learn two of the most powerful statements among traders, which are:

"Volatility isn't your enemy but your friend. Your best friend."

And

"You're only as good as the securities you trade."

Think of it this way, the only way you can make profitable day trades is when prices of securities go up or down during the day, depending on whether you're long or short. If prices are relatively flat, how can you hit your profit-taking price target?

Remember securities in play or SIP? Well, there are multiple ways to identify and select them. Some traders go for individual securities themselves, e.g., shares of stock of a particular company, a particular currency pair, or a particular cryptocurrency. Some trade a collection or package of securities, e.g., exchange-traded funds (ETFs). Some prefer to trade markets as a whole through securities like index futures contracts.

Remember, SIPs offer very good risk-reward ratio opportunities. And the good news is you can regularly monitor a SIP that may possibly go above or beyond its current market price because SIPs typically move frequently and with high levels of predictability.

There are new SIPs daily, which can give you opportunities to trade your funds optimally by providing very good risk-reward ratios during the day.

Securities in Play

What are stocks in play, again? They're securities that can be one or all of the following:

Securities that have significant new developments or news;

Securities whose prices are above or below the previous day's by at least 2% prior to market opening for the day;

Securities whose prices have moved significantly during the trading day; and

Securities with uncommon activities prior to market opening, keep in mind that when talking about securities with high trading volumes, we're talking about relative trading volume and not absolute trading volumes. What's the difference?

Let's compare two stocks, A and B. Stock A's average trading volume is 500,000 shares, while Stock B's average trading volume is 20 million shares. Stock B has a very high absolute trading volume compared to Stock A's daily average of only 500,000, which is considered low compared to Stock B's.

If Stock A's trading volume for the last 3 days between 900,000 to 1 million shares, while Stock B's trading volume for the same period was 22 million shares, Stock A has a higher relative trading volume for that period of time. Why?

Stock A's trading volume for the last three days is higher than its average by at least 400,000 shares, which is 80% of its average daily trading volume of 500,000 shares. Stock B's trading volume for the same period on the other hand, is higher than its daily average trading volume of 20 million shares by 2 million shares, which is only 10% of its average daily volume.

Because Stock A's trading volume for the last three days is up by at least 80% from its long-term daily average compared to only 10% for Stock B, Stock A has a very high relative trading volume compared to Stock B.

One of the reasons for choosing securities with high relative trading volume as compared to absolute trading volume is because more likely than not, low relative trading volume securities are being dominated by large trading institutions that use HFT computer programs, which retail day traders like us need to avoid.

When looking for high relative trading volume securities, remember that they need to be securities that trade independently from the entire market or their industry/sector. To get a general idea of how a particular security's market or sector's moving, just check out their major indexes. In the case of stocks, it's the Dow Jones Industrial Average or the S&P 500 index. When they're down, chances are that most stocks are down as well. When they're going up, chances are high that most stocks are going up as well.

Because high relative volume securities prices move independently from their respective markets, they're considered as securities in play or SIPs. There are only a few SIPs in the market every day, which are also referred to as "alpha" securities because they're on top of the list and nobody rules over them. Stick to such securities that have fundamental reasons or triggers for price movements for your day trading activities.

One of the things that set securities in motion or in play is freshly released and important news about or that can impact a particular security. And by freshly released, I mean the day before or during the trading day itself.

If it's stocks, it could be just-released corporate earnings or a newly-signed joint venture agreement with a major investor. It could also be news on the passage of a law that could restrict the business activities of that particular company. Such news can substantially impact investors' sentiment about that stock, which could make it move significantly in either direction.

Market Capitalization and Float

Float refers to the number of units of a particular security that's currently circulating or "floating" in the market. It could be the number of shares of stock of companies like Apple that are available in the market or the number of tokens of Bitcoin circulating on cryptocurrency exchanges.

Market capitalization refers to how much all of those shares or units in the market are worth. If there are 1 million shares of Stock A in circulating in the market today and its current market price is $5.00 per share, then Stock A's current market capitalization is $5 million, which will change accordingly as its stock prices goes up and down.

For optimal day trading purposes, low float and low market capitalization stocks are the way to go. Why?

Remember how volatility is a trader's best friend because it provides the profit opportunities that traders are looking for? Securities that have a bazillion units or shares floating in the market or have huge market capitalization (also called mega cap securities) are not likely to provide the volatility needed for profitable day trading. Why?

It would take a lot of units or shares and money to affect the prices significantly. The prices of securities that have low float and market capitalization (also called micro-cap securities) can be much more easily influenced because they neither need a lot of trading volume nor a lot of money to move.

And when looking for profitable day trading opportunities, you'll want to stick with securities that are volatile and not those that are steady.

For consistency purposes of discussions moving forward, I'll use stocks as financial securities that we'll day trade. This is because stocks are the most popular and easiest to understand financial security for day trading purposes.

Now that we've clarified that, let's take a look at three float categories of stocks that can be day traded:

Low float stocks that are less than $10 per share;

Medium float stocks that are between $10 to $100 per share; and

Mega cap stocks like Yahoo, Intel, Facebook, and Google, among others.

Stocks that have low float and are trading at less than $10 per share are very volatile. Just how volatile can they be? Their prices can swing by as much as 100% in a single trading day!

Because of their very high volatility, they provide the biggest potential for day trading profits. However, you must be very careful trading these stocks because they can swing the other way and much of your trading money in one fell swoop if you don't monitor them closely and act swiftly.

Because of their low float and prices, stocks under this category are very vulnerable to price manipulation by traders with a lot of trading ammo. As such, they can be very challenging for a newbie or inexperienced day traders. Because of the wild price swings, the chances of burning most of one's trading capital in a single day are high for newbie traders. Usually, only those with a whole lot of day trading experience and tools day trade stocks under this category.

Another thing to keep in mind with low float stocks below $10 per share is that they're not ideal for short-selling. Why?

One reason is that brokers are often reluctant to lend volatile stocks because of the high probability that prices spike rapidly and prevent those that borrow them from paying them back.

Another reason why such stocks aren't ideal is that their prices can swing wildly within a short period of time that it can wipe out a newbie day trader's account. If you want to minimize your day trading risks, especially as a newbie, it's best to leave this category of stocks to the experienced and sophisticated day traders for the meantime.

The second category of day trading stocks are medium float ones whose market prices hover between $10 to $100. By medium float, I mean around 10 to 500 million shares are circulating in the market. They provide just enough volatility to earn substantial money but not too volatile that newbie day traders are at high risk for losing most of their money in just one day.

The third category of stocks, the mega capitalized ones, have over half-a-billion shares floating in the market, which gives them a very huge market capitalization. So huge that only big, institutional traders can significantly impact their market prices.

This category should be off limits for retail day traders like you and I, unless there's a really good fundamental catalyst for moving their prices significantly within the day. But even then, it's best to avoid them as much as possible, considering that large institutional and HFT-powered traders dominate this category.

5. Trading Plan for Day Trading With Options

Build a Trade Plan

Set the Rules for Exit

One of the main mistakes that most traders fail to understand is that they usually concentrate over 80% of their efforts in trying to look for signals showing buy. They, however, fail to look at where and when they should exit a trade. Most investors will not risk selling if they are down because they are usually not ready for losses. You should get over it or else you will never make it in the trading world. Don't take things personally, especially when you are making losses. It only indicates that your predictions were incorrect. Keep it in mind that professional/experienced traders often have more losing trades that the winning trades. You will still make profits if you are able to manage your investments and limit your loses. Therefore before entering a trade, clearly know yours exists. For every trade you do, ensure that you have at least two exit points. The first exit point is the stop-loss which will tell you to exit in the event that you are trading negatively. You should ensure that you have a written exit spot and not memorizing them. Second, ensure that you have a profit target for each trade you perform. However, don't risk more than the percentage that you have set in your portfolio. Here are exit strategies you can choose;

Exit Strategy: Traditional Stop/Limit

The most effective way to keep your emotions in check is by setting targets or limits and stops the moment a trade is entered into. You can use the DailyFX to research into the over 4o million traders. You will realize that most of the successful traders set their risk to reward ratio to at least 1:1. Before entering into a market, you have to analyze the amount of risk you are willing to assume and then set a stop at this level, while at the same time, place your target at least many pips away. This means that if your predictions were wrong, your trade would be closed automatically, and this will be at an acceptable risk level. If your prediction is correct, the trade will be closed automatically after having your target. In either way, you will still have an exit.

Exit Strategy: Moving Average Trailing Stops

This exit strategy is also referred to as a moving average. This strategy is effective in filtering the direction a currency pair has trended. The main idea behind this strategy is that traders are usually busy looking for buying opportunities, particularly when the prices are above a moving average. Traders will also be busy looking for selling opportunities, especially when the prices are moving below the average. Therefore this strategy also considers the fact that a moving average can also be a trailing stop. This means that if a moving average cross over price, the trend is considered to be shifting. When you are a trend trader, you would consider closing out the position the moment a shift has occurred. It is preferred that you set your stop loss based on a moving average, as this is very effective.

Fig.1: Setting a trade exit using a moving average trailing stops

Exit Strategy: Volatility Bases Approach Using ATR
This technique involves the use of the Average True Range (ATR), which is designed to determine market volatility. It calculates the average range of the last 14 candles found between the high and low and thereby tells a trader the erratic behavior of the market. Traders can, therefore, use this to set stops and limits for every trade they do. A greater ATR on a given pair means a wider stop. This means if a volatile pair can generally be stopped out early, and thus will have a tight stop. You can adopt ATR for any time frame; a factor that makes to be considered as a universal indicator.

Set Entry Rules
We have set the exit rules to come before the entry rules for a reason. The reason is that exits are very

important compared to entries. The entry rule is basically simple. For instance, we can have an entry rule like: "Given that signal, B fires up and we have the minimum set target is suggested to be three times the stop loss, from the fact that we give that we at service, buying Y shares or contracts here is appropriated and allowed." In as much as the effectiveness of most of these systems are determined by how complicated they are, it should also be simple enough to enable you to make effective decisions quickly. In many cases, computers usually make better trade decisions than humans and this is the reason why nearly 50% of all trades occurring today are generated on computer programs.

Computers have powerful information processing capabilities and will not want to think or rely on emotions to make decisions. If a given condition is met, then they will automatically enter. They will exit when the trade hits its profit target or when the trade goes the wrong way. Each of the decisions made by a computer is based on probabilities. Otherwise, if you rely alone on your thoughts, it will difficult for you or almost impossible to make trades.

Building an effective watchlist requires three basic steps. The first step is collecting a handful of liquidity components of leadership in each of the major sectors in the market. Secondly, you will scan through stocks that meet the general technical criteria fitting your approach to the stock market. Third, do a rescan on the list nightly to be able to identify and locate setups or patterns that can generate opportunities in the session to follow while at the same time culling out the issues you don't have interest on may be due to their technical violations or secondary offerings, etc.

Building a Watch List

The U.S stock exchanges, for example, list more than 8,000 issues. However, a fund manager or a typical trader only accesses just a fraction. Why? Because they have failed to come up with their effective watch lists, the main reason behind this failure is because the identification of stocks that can fully support working strategies needs some skill sets, which is usually lacking in most participants. It is therefore wise that you learn this because it will mark a trading edge that is a lifetime. For you to have a well-organized watchlist, you should have a proper understanding of the modern market environment; you need to have an understanding of how different capitalization levels impact on price development. Lastly, you should also understand how different sectors are likely to react to different catalysts over time. When choosing the candidates you want to follow, be it on a daily, weekly, or monthly basis, you have to consider economic cycles, seasonality, and sentiments.

Guidelines for Building a Watchlist

The requirements of a watchlist depend on the amount of time a trader has to do trade and as well follow the financial markets. For instance, if you are a part-timer who only plays a few positions each week, daily, you can have a simple culling list having 50-100 issues to track. Otherwise, if you are a professional trader, you have to spend more time on the task. You should build a primary database containing 350 - 500 stocks. You should also have a secondary list fitting your trading screens. Note that each trading screen should be able to accommodate between 20 and 75 issues, but this will depend on the space that charts, market depth, scanners, and news stickers' windows will take. It is appropriate that to trade well, one screen should be devoted to stickers and each entry of these stickers should display just a maximum of three fields like the percentage change, the last price, and the net change. Try to link these stickers as this will enable you to have a quick review of price patterns, particularly during the trading day.

Execution

This refers to the completion of a sell or buys of an order for a security. Order execution occurs when the order gets filled and not when an order is placed by an investor. As an investor, when you submit the trade, the trade is sent to a broker. The broker determines the best way with which this trade can be executed. The law requires that brokers give the best execution possible to the investors. There is an established commission, referred to as the Securities and Exchange Commission, where brokers report the quality of their executions. Brokers are also required to notify customers whose orders were not routed for best execution. The growth of online brokers today has made the cost of trade execution to reduce significantly. Today, many traders offer a commission rebate to their customers for some set monthly targets for these customers. This can be very important for the short-term trader who tries to keep the execution costs low as possible.

There are high probabilities that you will be able to settle at the desired price if you have placed a market order or any other order that is relatively easy to be converted into a market order. However, this does not apply for all cases because there are orders that may be too large and will require that they be broken down to come up with several small orders and this might be very difficult to execute and get the best possible price range. To solve this, you can involve the use of risk in the system. Execution risk is the lag between order placement and settlement.

How Did I Do It?

Trading is a business and for you to succeed in trading, you have to treat it just the same way you would have treated any other business. As a trader, all does not stop with having knowledge on where the market has the potential to rise or fall or when to pause or reverse but rather a trader must be able to precisely determine what exact market event is going to take place and act accordingly. While trading, you have a well-written plan that is subjected to re-evaluation after the closing of a market. Your plan must be able to change with the changing market conditions. So be an individual who can adjust and improve your trading skills. Your plan as a trader should take into account your personal trading goals and styles. Never use another person's trading plan as this will not reflect your characteristics. A successful trade must begin by building a perfect master plant. A good trading plan will include the following;

Set Your Risk Levels
Ask yourself the risk you can handle in any trade you make. However, this is determined by your risk tolerance and trading style. On any given trading day, your portfolio should have a risk tolerance ranging between 1% - 5%. This means that on any trading day, if you happen to lose an amount that is in that range, you will get out of the trade. It is always better to fight another day.

Set Goals
An effective trader sets realistic profit targets before entering any trade. You have to assess the minimum

risk/reward ratios you can accept. As observed, most pro traders will always not accept to take a trade unless the potential profit that the trade will yield is at least twice or thrice the risk. A good scenario is a case where you have a dollar loss per share in your stop-loss; therefore, your goal will be making a $3 profit. Be precise; ensure that you set your weekly, monthly and at large your annual profit goal either in as a percentage or in dollars of your trade portfolio. Regularly re-assess these goals.

6. Red to Green Trading Strategy with Options in Day Trading

If you are looking for another easy to work with trading strategies, the red to green option is a good one to work with. This one will rely on the information from the previous day close to help you figure out where the stock will go and what decisions you need to make.

While looking at this information, if you notice that the current price of the stock is higher than it was on the previous stay, this means that the market is moving from what is called a green day to a red day. This means that the percentage that the price has changed will now be negative, which will be shown as red in most of the platforms that you look at. This is known as a green to red move.

On the other hand, if the price is lower than what you found on the previous day, this means that the market is moving from a red day to a green day. This means that the percentage that the price has changed will be positive now, which will be shown as green in color on most platforms. This will be considered a red to green move.

You will find that this will be a strategy that is pretty much the same whether you are working with green to red and for red to green, except for the direction that the trade is going or whether it is long or short. So, to keep things simple here, we will just stick with one of them and use the same rules for both of them.

To summarize the strategy that you would like to use with trading the red to green strategy, you would go with the following steps:

• When you are creating your watchlist for the day, you will want to take a look at the previous day close and then monitor the price action at that time.

• If you see that the stock is moving towards where it was at the previous day close with a high volume, it is time to consider going long, using the profit target that occurred on the close of the previous day.

• The stop loss that you will use will be the nearest technical level. This means that if you buy near the VWAP, the stop loss will be when there is a break of the VWAP. If you are buying near a moving average or an important support level, you will want to place the stop loss near the break of the support level or the moving average.

• It is a good idea to sell at the profit target. If the price ends up moving in your favor, it is time to consider bringing the stop loss up the break-even point and then make sure to not let this price go against you. When you are done with that, the red to green move should start working right away.

You will be able to use an approach in a similar way if you want to work on the green to red strategy because they work pretty much the same way.

7. Bull and Bear Put Spread Strategy with Options in Day Trading

Bull Put Spread

If you would like to work with a bull put strategy, some of the things that you will need to do include:

Select the stock or the index that fits the criteria for trading on this strategy. This is going to be based on your medium or short-term outlook for that stock.

You will then sell one OTM put option of this stock. Buy one OTM put option that has the same expiry date and the same underlying stock as the put option that you did in the second step, but you will pick a lower strike price.

Once you are done with the above steps, you should make sure to monitor your position the whole time and then close both the options at the same time once the trade has made a good profit. Alternately, you can choose to hold onto the trade until both options reach their expiration, which can help you to get the maximum profit. You will only want to go to the expiration day if you feel confident that the stock does not have any threat of following below the strike price of your higher strike put option ahead of time.

When should I use this strategy?

The first question that you may have about this strategy is when you would choose to use this kind of strategy. You will want to use this kind of spread when you believe that your underlying stock has gotten to a strong support level and there isn't much of a chance that the stock will go down much from that level, at least before the chosen expiration date.

A good time to choose this kind of trade is when the stock has just gone through some expected correction or a profit booking. For example, it may be a strong stock that underwent a decline of about five percent, and then it started to show that it was stabilizing again at the lower level. You do need to make sure that the buying volume and the number of buyers is the same or increasing so that the stock is likely to go back up rather than down. Or you can pick to start trading when a stock is slowly climbing up and it doesn't seem likely that it is going to fall back down in the near-term.

For this strategy, it is preferable for you to trade options that are historically low in volatility. This is a credit spread strategy that will exploit the time-decay. when working with low-volatility stocks, a price fall is only going to be small and this makes it unlikely to overcome the time-decay of the options. Basically, this keeps the trade profitable, even if the stock doesn't move with your expectations. This strategy can sometimes work for the higher-volatility stocks as well if the opportunity presents itself, but this is not always the best choice to go with.

Advantages and disadvantages

The biggest advantage of using the bull put spread strategy is that it will make sure that the time-decay will work in your favor. Even if your stock doesn't go up after it hits the support level and it stays stagnant, you will be able to get gain because of the time-decay. in addition, if you use this strategy in times of high volatility in the market, any drop is going to act like a catalyst in making the trade profitable at a faster rate.

The biggest disadvantage of using this kind of strategy is that the maximum amount of profit that you are able to earn is less than the potential that you could use if the stock doesn't go the way that you would like and your positions get into losses.

A Case Study for the Bull Put Spread Trade

We are going to look here at an actual trade that was done successfully to show you how this strategy works. we are going to enter the market on April of 2017 and use the stock known as Biocon Limited as our underlying stock.

First, we took some time to determine the optimum strike prices to trade on. To do this, we need to determine a put option to sell that had a delta that was no more than -0.25. this means that the trade had the right balance of probability and potential profit and it implies that right now there is only a 25 percent chance of the option ending ITM at expiry. What all this means is that this option is going to give us a 75 percent chance or more of success when a decent premium is collected.

The next step that you need to do is sell the OTM put option. You can then buy a lower-strike OTM put option of the same stock using the same expiry date. For the first part, you would see that the Biocon 1100 put option in April was sold for about $4.70. Then for the second part, the Biocon 1080 put option was bought for $1.75 to complete this part of the trade.

Summary Table		
Stock or Index Traded	Biocon	
Lot Size for option	100	
Option 1	Strike Price	1,100.00
(Higher strike OTM Put : Sell)	Premium Received	4.70
Option 2	Strike Price	1,080.00
(Lower strike OTM Put : Buy)	Premium Paid	1.75
Difference Between any 2 Consecutive Strikes prices		20.00
Potential Max Profit		1,770.00
Potential Max Loss		10,230.00
Condition for meeting max profit	Stock/Index price at expiry >=	1,100
Condition for meeting max loss	Stock/Index price at expiry <=	1,080
Break-Even	Stock/Index Price at expiry =	1,097

This tabulation is going to show you how much profit you can potentially make if the Biocon stayed over the 1100. At the end of the day, the maximum amount is $1770. In addition, it shows the maximum amount that you can lose even if the stock went below the lower-strike price, which is $10,230. The point for breaking even, which means the point above which the trade would still provide you with a profit is $1097.05. Historically for this option, the delta values of the options you are trading will have less than 20 percent chance of ending in a loss, which fits into the amount that we wanted earlier.

This chart below is going to be the profit and loss payoff diagram is going to show the profits and losses that you can get as they are plotted against the five different expiry prices for this stock.

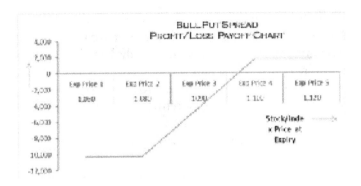

Results of this trade

Even though this stock is showing some fluctuations from one day to another, it still ended up at 1123 at the end of the day. Therefore, both options expired worthless as OTM options that resulted in an overall profit for this trade.

This trade yielded a profit of $1770. This was also the maximum that the trader cold potentially makes off the trade and was equal to the new premium that was received when the trader entered the trade. Since both options ended up expiring at $0, the traded realized maximum returns.

The ratio of the net profit or loss to the sum invested in the trade will help you to figure out your return on investment, or the amount of profit that you earned on this trade. In this example, a sum of $86,000 was blocked off by the broker as the margin to sell the 1100 Biocon put option that was sold for a total of $2820 and the trader paid $1050 for the purchasing power of the lower-strike put option. This means that the total investment for this trade ended up being $87,050 and the profit was $1770.

With these numbers, the profit ration ends up being 0.02, or about two percent. This is not a bad return on investment given that this trade only lasted six hours. The longer you are going to hold onto the option, the higher the risk is going to be to you, so you would probably want to go with a return on investment that is a little bit higher. But for this short of a time, you made some money and that is not too bad!

Bear Put Spread

To get started with this kind of strategy, you will want to pick out the right stock that will fit into the criteria that is needed for this strategy. Remember that for this strategy, you want to have a negative outlook on the chosen stock. You want a stock that is going to go down for some reason, whether you have heard some bad news about the stock or there is something else that is going to bring the value of your stock down.

After you have been able to pick out the right stock, you will need to purchase one slightly OTM put option. You will also want to sell one OTM put option, making sure that the strike price ends up being about one or two strikes lower than the option that you purchased in the first step. You also want to make sure that you are picking out ones that have the same stock and the same expiry date as what you did with the first step.

Once you are done with all these trades, you want to make sure that you monitor your position and watch what is going on. You will then want to get out of both positions once they have helped you to receive significant profit, which is about 30 to 40 percent of maximum potential profit.

This one is going to work like what you were able to do with the bull call spread. If you decide to increase the spread, you are going to increase how much potential profit you can make, but it also increases the risks that you are dealing with. In addition, you can choose to decrease the spread, the risk will also decrease, but you would also limit how much profit you could potentially make on the trade.

There are a few times when you will choose to trade using the bear put spread. You will want to go with this kind of strategy when the market has a pretty negative outlook on the stock that you want to use. This is usually going to happen when some development occurs, such as the company not making the earnings that it should, or the organization has made some new changes or decisions that the investors did not look at favorably.

Some people choose to trade with this kind of strategy when the company is part of or is selling under pressure. They do not want to sell but there is something that is going on that will make them feel like they do need to sell. For example, there may be some environment or market conditions that are unfavorable to the company that surfaced and is changing the company.

Remember that since the bear put spread is considered a debit spread strategy, you will have to work with the time-decay and it is going to go against your overall position, even though this kind of decay is considered a lot of slower than what will happen with a naked long put position.

When it comes to the disadvantages and advantages, this spread is going to end up being pretty like the bull call spread. The primary advantage that comes with this trade is that ratio for risk and reward is pretty good and even a moderate decrease on a stock can still help you to earn some good profits.

You will also be able to increase the amount of profit that you could potentially make by widening up the spread. To do this, you will want to increase the strike price that happens between your two options. You can also choose to reduce your risk in order to help you out as a beginner and to do this you will decrease the spread. In order to decrease the risk, you will want to decrease the number of strike prices that are going on between the two options.

The biggest disadvantage that comes with this strategy is dealing with the time decay that will work against the position. And while there is a limited amount of potential loss, if the stock ends up staying stagnant for a long period of time, the position is going to end up with a loss.

8. Technical Analysis Indicators for Options in Day Trading

A day trader who can acknowledge a pattern on the charts can figure out where costs are probably to go up until some unpredicted occasion occurs that produces a brand-new pattern. Technical analysis is the tool that assists a day trader to identify those patterns.

Technical analysis is the research study of market information to anticipate the instructions of future rate motions. Along with simple research, the method is conceived of as a branch of protection research. Here we look at how technological modelling can be seen in day-trading.

In a lot of markets, every day produces a brand-new bar (lots of traders discuss bars rather of days, and they aren't discussing where they pursue work). A collection of bars, with all their various high, low, open, and close points, is created into a bigger chart. Typically, a plot of the volume for each bar runs beneath.

Numerous patterns formed in the charts are connected with future rate relocations. Technical experts, therefore, invest a great deal of time taking a look at the charts to see whether they can anticipate what is going to occur. When particular technical patterns take place so that the traders can position orders appropriately, lots of software application plans send out traders signals.

The plots form patterns that can be examined to reveal what occurred. How did the supply and need for a security modification, and why? And what does that mean for future supply and need?

A couple of market individuals want to go that far. However, they yield the point that the rate is the single essential summary of details about a business. That suggests that technical analysis, taking a look at how the rate modifications in time, is a method of discovering whether a security's potential customers are enhancing or becoming worse.

1. Presumptions in Technical Analysis

While some financiers and traders utilize both technical and basic analysis, most tend to fall under one camp or another or a minimum of depending on one much more greatly in making trading choices.

Macro-level basic analysis requires the research study or forecasting of financial development, inflation, credit cycles, rates of interest patterns, capital circulations in between nations, labor and resource usage and their cyclicality, market patterns, reserve bank and political policies and habits, geopolitical matters, customer and organization patterns, and "soft" information (e.g., belief or self-confidence studies).

Many big banks and brokerages have groups that focus on both technical and essential analysis. In basic, the more quality details one takes in to enhance the chances of being right, the much better one's trading outcomes are most likely to be.

Technical analysis is based upon the property that securities rates relocate patterns which those patterns duplicate themselves in time. Details about the cost, time, and volume of a security's trading can be outlined on a chart.

It frequently contrasts with basic analysis, which can be used both on a macroeconomic and microeconomic level. The micro-level essential analysis consists of the research study of incomes, expenses, liabilities, possessions and revenues, capital structure, and "soft" aspects (quality of management group, competitive position).

The standard component of technical analysis is a bar, which reveals you the high, low, open, and closing cost of security for an offered day.

Technical analysis is a method to determine the supply and need in the market. It's a tool for evaluating the marketplaces, not forecasting them. Everybody would be able to make cash in the markets if analyzing the significance of the information were that simple.

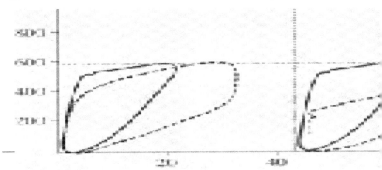

2. Volume modifications

The standard bar demonstrates how rate altered throughout the day, however including volume details informs the other part of the story: just how much of security was required at that cost. If the need is increasing, then more individuals desire security, so they want to pay more for it. The rate informs traders what the marketplace understands; the volume informs them the number of individuals in the market understands it.

Changes to home flooring	25,868	3	1,903	11,580
			(8.7%)	(61.8%)
Door widening	34,408	1,775	17,413	7,434
		(5.2%)	(50.7%)	(21.6%)
Electric bed	33,437	13,264	5,250	8,554
		(39.7%)	(15.0%)	(25.6%)
Handrail & Grab rail	1,277	290	607	0
		(22.6%)	(47.6%)	
Hoist	43,718	5,802	25,498	0
		(17.5%)	(58.3%)	
Ramps	75,780	4,403	45,367	18,020
		(5.8%)	(60.5%)	(23.4%)
Specialised Mattress	9,400	5,400	600	1,884
		(57.4%)	(6.4%)	(20.0%)
Stair Lift	4,985	500	991	1,988
		(17.7%)	(24.9%)	(11.5%)
Stair rail	785	327	181	262
		(41.7%)	(16.7%)	(11.4%)
Extensive home improvement	190,000	3	143,000	11,000
			(71.9%)	(0.5%)

3. Cost modifications

Market observer's argument market performance all the time. In an effective market, all info about security is currently consisted of in the security's cost, so there's no indicate doing any research study at all.

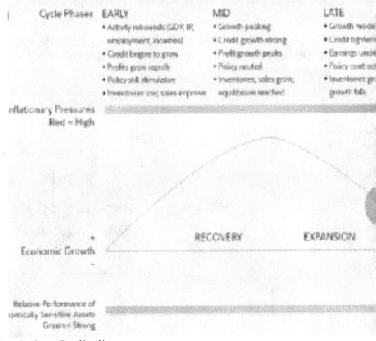

4. Market Cyclicality

Humanity being what it is, with typically shared behavioral attributes, market history tends to duplicate itself. The series of occasions is not apt to duplicate itself completely. However, the patterns are usually comparable. These can take the kind of short-term or long-lasting rate habits.

Another presumption behind technical analysis (and all securities analysis more broadly) is that cost does stagnate according to a "random walk", or according to no rational or noticeable pattern. Rather it moves according to patterns that are both foreseeable and explainable.

Technical analysis alone cannot completely or properly anticipate the future; it is beneficial to recognize patterns, behavioral predispositions, and prospective inequalities in supply and need where trading chances might develop.

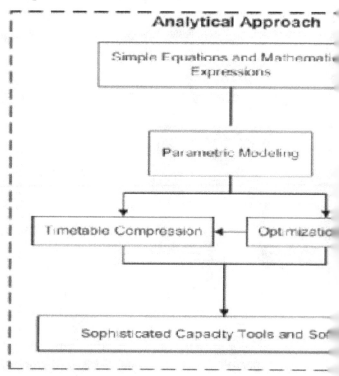

5. Analytical Approaches

There are numerous methods to approach technical analysis. The most basic technique is through a fundamental candlestick cost chart, which reveals cost history and the purchasing and offering characteristics of cost within a given duration.

Initially, technical analysis was mainly a matter of "checking out the tape" or analyzing the succeeding circulation and magnitude of cost and volume information through a stock ticker. As computer systems ended up being more extensive in the 1970s, information was assembled into chart kind and ended up being a service technician's basic point of recommendation.

Acknowledgement of chart patterns and bar analysis were the most typical kinds of analysis, followed by regression analysis, moving averages, and rate connections. Today, the variety of technical signs is far more. Anybody with coding understanding appropriate to the software application can change rate or volume information into a specific indication of interest.

Others use a cost chart together with technical indications or utilize specific kinds of technical analysis, such as Elliott wave theory or harmonics, to produce trade concepts. Some usage parts of a number of various approaches. At the exact same time, traders need to withstand the concept of "details overload" or jumbling charts with numerous signs and lines that it starts to negatively affect one's capability to check out the chart.

6. Candlestick

Candlestick charts are the most typical type of charting in today's software application. Green (or in some cases white) is typically utilized to illustrate bullish candle lights, where the existing rate is greater than the opening cost. Red (or often black) prevails for bearish

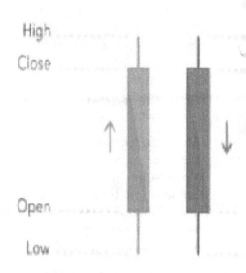

candle lights, where present cost is listed below the opening cost.

When particular guidelines evenly use to enhance the neutrality of their trading and prevent psychological predispositions from affecting its efficiency, others might get in into trades just.

Traders might take a subjective judgment to their trading calls, preventing the requirement to trade based upon a limiting rules-based technique provided the originality of each circumstance.

Overlay indications are positioned over the initial rate chart.

Moving Average-- A pattern line that alters based upon brand-new cost inputs. A 50-day basic moving average would represent the typical cost of the previous 50 trading days. Rapid moving averages weight the line more greatly towards current rates.

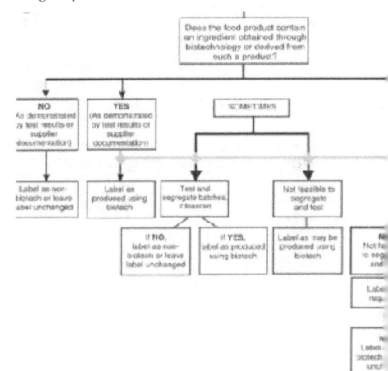

7. Non-Chart Based.

Not all technical analysis is based upon charting or arithmetical improvements of cost. Some technical experts depend on sentiment-based studies from organizations and customers to assess where the rate may be going.

Heiken-Ashi charts utilize candlesticks as the outlining medium; however, take the various mathematical formula of cost. Rather of the guideline of candle lights equated from standard open-high-low-close requirements, rates are smoothed too much better show trending cost action according to this formula.

Breakout-- When cost breaches a location of assistance or resistance, frequently due to a significant rise in offering or purchasing volume.

It reveals the range in between the opening and closing costs (the body of the candlelight) and the overall day-to-day variety (from top of the wick to bottom of the wick).

Rate action-- The motion of rate, as graphically represented through a chart of a specific market.

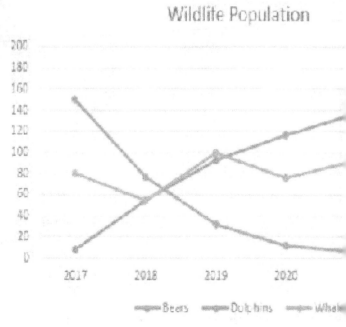

8. Line chart.

Pattern-- Price motion that continues one instruction for an extended time period.

Resistance-- A rating level where a prevalence of sell orders might lie, triggering cost to bounce off the level downward. Enough purchasing activity, typically from increased volume, is typically needed to breach it.

Bollinger Bands-- Uses a basic moving typical and plots two lines two basic discrepancies above and listed below it to form a variety. Frequently utilized by traders utilizing a mean reversion technique where rate moving above or listed below the bands is "extended" and possibly anticipated to revert back inside the bands.

Ichimoku Cloud-- Designed to be an "all-in-one" sign that offers assistance and resistance, momentum, pattern, and creates trading signals.

If the market is exceptionally bullish, this may be taken as an indication that nearly everybody is totally invested and a couple of purchasers stay on the sidelines to press rates up even more. This may recommend that costs are more likely to trend down.

Favorable Volume Index-- Typically utilized along with the unfavorable volume index, the indication is created to reveal when institutional financiers are most active under the facility they're probably to offer or purchase when the volume is low. When volume is up from the previous day, focuses on days.

On-Balance Volume-- Uses volume to anticipate subsequent modifications in rate. Advocates of the sign location credence into the concept that if volume modifications with a weak response in the stock, the cost relocation is most likely to follow.

Advance-Decline Line-- Measures the number of stocks advanced (gotten in worth) in an index vs the variety of stocks that decreased (declined). If an index has actually gotten in worth, however just 30% of the stocks are up however 70% are down or neutral, that's an indicator that the purchasing is most likely just taking place in particular sectors instead of being favorable towards the whole market.

Product Channel Index (CCI) -- Identifies cyclical conditions or brand-new patterns.

Momentum-- The rate of modification in rate with regard to time.

Retracement-- A turnaround in the instructions of the dominating pattern, anticipated to be short-term, typically to a level of assistance or resistance.

Doji-- A candlelight type defined by little or no modification in between the close and open rate, revealing indecision in the market.

Stochastic Oscillator-- Shows the present rate of the security or index relative to the low and high rates from a user-defined variety. They were utilized to identify overbought and oversold market conditions.

Channel-- Two parallel pattern lines set to imagine a combination pattern of specific instructions. A breakout above or listed below a channel might be translated as an indication of a possible trading and a brand-new pattern chance.

Momentum-- The rate of modification of cost with regard to time.

Typical Directional Movement Rating (ADXR) -- Measures the rate of modification in a pattern.

A worth listed below one is thought about bullish; a worth above one is thought about bearish. Volume is determined in the variety of shares traded and not the dollar quantities, which is a main defect in the sign (prefers lower price-per-share stocks, which can sell greater volume). It is however still shown on the flooring of the New York Stock Exchange. (Of advancing stocks/ of decreasing stocks)/ (volume of advancing stocks/ volume of decreasing stocks).

Arms Index (aka TRIN) -- Combines the variety of stocks decreasing or advancing with their volume according to the formula.

Coppock Curve-- Momentum indication, at first meant to recognize bottoms in stock indices as part of a long-lasting trading technique.

9. Secrets of Day Trading Options

Are there day-to-day business secrets that will revolutionize the way you trade? Surely not! Trading is stressful and hard work. Many people want a trading service that tells them when to get into and out of business. Deal warnings are useful if you know why you take the deal.

Nonetheless, few positive moves to take when you deal in the day, you will visit us in our daytime trading room every day to hear us talk about what's happening in real-time. We already have a trading watch list of our days that we set out every day. If the economy is so weak, of course, there would be no decent configurations. It is essential not to push trades in indecision mode while the market is open. Trading tricks of the day are not going to support you in an indecisive environment. Every trader should have its unique trading style, specialty investment region, and collection of rules or guidelines. There are nevertheless a few main day trading tips that any great trader faithfully knows and practices. Given all the possible differences between traders, trading has a few things that are completely important to success. Price action is one of the most common business principles. A trader who knows how to manipulate market behavior, the correct way will also significantly boost his efficiency and the way he looks at charts.

However, a lot of misunderstandings and half-truths still circulate which confuse traders and set them up for failure. Too many merchants struggle in volume and fail to sit down and look at the price of their companies. And ignore the urge to find out where they are going wrong and why. That is why I keep a log of Trade

Bench to the top of my secrets of day trading of commodities or some other device.

Trade Bench is an online business journal that is entirely open. You should schedule trades, place sizes, and the risk management platform goes with it. More notably, it maintains a precise log of past deals, including Entry & Exit points Trading Period of Open & Close Place value Profit/loss, which helps you to look back and find competitive vulnerabilities quickly. While some will try to make the same errors, you will be improving steadily. Knowledge is Power an occurrence on the other side of the globe will quickly impact the business with instant contact. Therefore it is important than ever to have access to credible news outlets. Many services, though, go beyond covering the breaking news. They also offer detailed analysis and commentary. It will all improve your ability to predict potential market change. Therefore, Financial Juice is one of the best-hidden secrets of day trading. If you have signed up for a free user account, live news can be read out audibly when they crack—staying up to date with developments that can have a precise and effortless effect on the business. All of this make it one of the best day trading secrets to be revealed. Economic Calendars the next of our day trading secrets to be disclosed is a device that traders sometimes forget, an economic calendar. They track market driving things happening. These will also allow you to predict and arrange a schedule for a potential event when used appropriately.

But, generally speaking, using an economic calendar is not the best-kept secret. Instead, the device Price Warning is used as it is.

Reasons to Use Day Trading Options

Day Trading options, you need to know what they are first. A choice is a deal between a seller and a vendor involving a specific stock or other investment. The option holder has the right to compel the option seller to do as the contract specifies within the time-limit determined by the deal. When the buyer exercises power, the seller must obey the option's directions.

For example, call option on a stock offers the buyer choose the right to purchase a certain amount of shares at any point before a stated expiration date at a predetermined price. If the buyer uses the power, the right seller must sell the stock to the buyer option. The most critical feature of an offer is that the holder of the offer retains the right to execute the deal, as the name implies, but is under no duty to do so. The buyer choice should then only use this right when it is wise to do so. Assume the call option has allowed the buyer to pay $100 per share for a given stock. If the stock sold in the market for $50 per share, the option holder would never use the right, because it would be dumb to spend $100 on the free market under the reason for a stock the investor might purchase for $50. Nevertheless, if the market share price is $175, then the buyer would pursue the right because $100 would be a steal over the current share price.

There are several different methods of using the options for trading. Besides, to call options as mentioned above, put options give the buyer option the right to sell stock at a specified price, thus shielding the buyer option from losses in a portfolio. You should also mix various call and put options to take advantage of more advanced options approaches that can make a profit in several circumstances.

There are two key reasons that an investor should use the options for trading: Speculation and hedge.

Speculation you might think of thought as betting on a security campaign. The value of options is that you're not limited to profiting even when the demand is rising.

Use options that way are the reason that prospects have a reputation for being unpredictable. Why? For what? If you buy an alternative, you need to be accurate in deciding not only the direction of movement of the stock but also the extent and timing of this transfer. For the win, you have to forecast accurately whether the stock will go up or down, and you have to be accurate about how much the demand will change as well as the timeframe it will take for all of this to happen. And also don't forget the fees!

So why do people speculate on choices when the chances are too skewed? Apart from flexibility, the use of the leverage is all about. When you control 100 shares with one contract, it does not take much of a price move to generate significant profits.

A hedging position would almost certainly be lower than the primary stake. Still, if the hedging stake was obtained on better terms, a hedge will also render a lost transaction lucrative.

Hedges in Day Trading Options

Hedging is a practice that many investors, and not just options traders, often use. The underlying theory of the strategy is that, when taking another position, it is used to minimize or remove the chance of holding one specific investment position. The flexibility of contract options makes them especially useful when it comes to hedging, and they are widely used to this end. Options traders also use choices to hedge against a decline in the price of a single option, or equity portfolio that they hold. By taking up an opposing position, traders in options will hedge current positions.

Hedging the other function is to hedge options. Find that to be an insurance scheme. Much when you protect your home or vehicle, opportunities will be used to protect against a loss on your assets. Supporters of options say you shouldn't take the money because you're so uncertain about your stock choice that you need a hedge. By using alternatives, you'd be able to mitigate the downside cost-effectively while enjoying the full upside.

Advantage of Price Movements

Price action is one of the most common business principles. A trader who knows how to manipulate market behavior, the correct way will also significantly boost his efficiency and the way he looks at charts. However, a lot of misunderstandings and half-truths still circulate which confuse traders and set them up for failure. In this post, we discuss the eight most critical secrets of price action and share the best tips for price action. Whenever the price hits a point of encouragement or opposition, the equilibrium between buyers and sellers varies. Each time the price hits resistance during an upward trend, more buyers enter the market and expand their sales business. When the demand hits the same amount of strength again, there will be fewer buyers waiting. This effect is also known as the absorption of order. The resistance is slowly reduced until consumers no longer face opposition, and the market will break upward and begin the path uphill. To grasp the dynamics of price and candlestick, it helps if you picture the fluctuations of prices in financial markets as a war between buyers and sellers. Buyers hope that with their purchases or purchase interest, the rates would increase and push the market higher. Sellers are banking on dropping rates and making their sales value drive the price down. Whether one hand is better than the other, the stock markets will see the following trends emerging. Whether there are many buyers than sellers or more purchasing interest than selling value, investors have no one from whom they will purchase. The prices then increase until the demand gets so high that the sellers find it enticing to get interested once again. Around the same time, inevitably, the market is too high for the consumers to keep buying. If more sellers than buyers, though, prices should decline before equilibrium is restored, and more customers are joining the market. The more significant the gap between these two business participants, the further the economy is heading in one direction.

Nonetheless, rates continue to adjust more gradually because there is just a small overhang. There is no need to change the price while the purchasing and selling preferences are in equilibrium. Both sides are satisfied with the present rate, and business equilibrium occurs.

It is also necessary to bear that in mind because every pricing research seeks to compare the power ratio of the two sides to determine which market actors are better and thus in which direction the demand is most likely to rise.

10.Create Passive Income with Day Trading

Before you start trading, look around the market and make your plan on which combination of currencies will you trade. This depends on the volatility of their exchange prices, which is based on previous research done on the past profitable exchanges. Planning also includes the time that you are willing to sit down and monitor the trades, make sure that you stick to the time scheduled to avoid messing up the already earned profit. Remember that choosing the time to trade should be at a time when the market is more active. The market will be there tomorrow and, therefore, when your scheduled time closes your trades. Strategy to be used throughout the time you are trading should also be thought out before you start trading, and it should be adhered to throughout the trading period in the day.

When day trading, you have to know how to manage your money because at the end of the day you want to have money, not lose money. During the day, you will take part in several trades, and therefore you need to know the amount of money you will use to invest. You have to prepare for losses and gains, but the total loss you expect is of importance to avoid losing all your money at the end of the day. This starts by knowing the risk per trade; this is the amount of money you are ready to lose on one trade. If you are a beginner, it is good to set your risk at a maximum of 2%. The size of the account should also be taken into account. If you have a trade that according to you, has a stop-loss of close to 50 pips, if you risk $200, your risk will be $4. This is done by dividing the amount of money you are risking by the stop loss pips.

Always have a stop target before you start trading, and also consider the type of market you are trading in; there are markets that are so dynamic such that your stop order might not be executed as per the set value. Therefore, to be safe, set your stops using the actual price-action and the conditions prevailing in the market, it is good to set them around the resistance, and support levels, chart patterns, trend lines, and how volatile the currencies you are using are in the market. It is not only the stop loss position that you should consider during day trading, but also consider the point at which you want to take profits. For maximum profit, place appropriate levels of taking profit.

In addition, you should look at the reward-risk ratio, and when it is 1:1, it means that the amount you are risking equal to what you expect as a profit, and 3:1 has a triple amount to gain to lose. You can mix these such trades such that you have many with a high potential of gaining and few with an equal potential of winning. You can do it the other way around, but make sure that there is a balance that will leave you with some profit.

Although trading takes place at all times in the world, each market region has its own hours of trade. Therefore, as a trader, you should know your market, and it's opening and closing hours. You should also know that trading is not good throughout a trading day, and trading is good when the market activity is high. We have four major trading markets, and each of them has its own opening and closing hours. However, there are markets that open around the same time. For example, Tokyo market open at 7 P.M and close at 4 A.M while the Sydney market opens at 5 P.M until 2 A.M looking at the opening hours of the two markets, there is a time when they are all open, and the, therefore, the level of activity with the currencies increases in the two markets between 5 P.M and 8 P.M when you are in the two markets, it is the best time to trade. This means that when more than one market is open at the same time, the trading activities are heightened, and the price of currencies fluctuates more. Therefore, maximize this by doing trades during the time when the market is very active.

You should also be alert on any news release that can make the price of the currency to fluctuate as you look out for changes in prices. Remember that the news can go against the predicted trend, and if you had already taken a position, you can either lose or gain, and it happens in seconds. You can make money by reacting correctly and within the correct time in day trading. The news to look out for is the GDP data, trade deficits, central bank meetings and announcements, consumer confidence, among other big news affecting the economy in the region.

As you look out for the fluctuations in prices, stay in check not to open so many trades that you cannot control. Having many trades does not mean that you will get a lot of money. The best thing to do is to start your trade-in small portions. Identify three trades that show potential and monitor the trends; it is good to deal with two trades in a day that you will maximize on their profits than dealing with many that you will not make money on.

The amount of money made in the day also depends on the type of trading strategy used. To make more money choose a trading system that will give you more. When using scalping, it can help you to gain more, but you should increase the number of trades because the income obtained from one trade is very small. This is done when your main strategy is scalping. You can do more than one hundred trades in a day so that at the end of the day you have many wins than losses thus at the end of the day you have good money in your wallet.

If you are doing scalping as a supplementary strategy, you should use it when the market is not giving a large range in terms of the fluctuation of prices of currencies. In this case, most of the time, there are no trends in a longer time frame, and therefore using scalping in the short time frame becomes the best option to exploit. This way, you are assured that even without visible trends, there is a possibility that you will not end the day without money. This means that you initiate a long time frame trade, and as it develops, you start new sets of trade with a shorter time frame; it should be done in the same direction. You will then be entering and leaving the trade, as you collect small amounts, then later get a major profit with the long time frame.

In a day, you can also use the false breakouts to make money in day trading. Looking at a trend, you can spot a breakout that you believe that it will not maintain the same direction. This is when you make a move, when the trend comes back to its original line; using this quick realization, you can make some cash. Using a fading breakout is the most effective because breakout tends to come out and out, and eventually, they succeed, but with a fading breakout, you will be sure of making money. The rationale of using breakouts is that the resistance and support levels are known as ceilings and price floors respectively, and when one of them is broken, traders expect the trend to continue in that direction and therefore, the traders react in the opposite direction, which later stabilizes the trend to its original flow. An example is that when the resistance level is broken, most traders think that the price will continue in the upward trend and buy the currency instead of selling. You should, therefore, sell the currency, acting contrary to what everyone is doing, and when the breakout returns to normal, you buy again at a lower price. Similarly, when the support is broken, it means that the movement of the price is downwards, and most traders are likely to sell and not buy. To collect funds from this move, you should buy the currency instead of selling, and when the price resumes to its trend line, you sell it out. This type of trading is much profitable, but it can be very risky, therefore, analyze the graph well to make sure that it is a false breakdown before you enter the trade. However, to be safer, place a limit order when buying and selling, and make sure that at the end of the day, you have money in your wallet.

You can also make money using pivot points, which helps you to determine how prices of currencies are moving. Most of the time, the pivot points will identify prices as bullish or bearish, then represent the averages for the low, high prices and closing prices occurring on a trading day. Do you need to know the market trend? The pivot points will help you with that. Use the pivot points to determine the general direction of the trade; if the market price of the currency is above the base of the pivot point, it suggests that the trade is bullish, and when it is below the pivot base, then it is bearish. In addition, when using pivot points, close all the long position trades when the market gets to the resistance levels and close the short ones when the market goes below the support level.

There is also the use of a reversal strategy that is commonly used around the globe; this strategy will help you to make money within a very short time, especially if the currency is moderately volatile. To use this strategy, you will have to study the graph to determine whether it has several consecutive highs and lows. At the highest point, which is called the top, you can easily predict that the price of the currency will reverse, and then react immediately by selling the currency. Similarly, if the graph of the currency has the lowest point, which is known as the bottoms, you predict that the trend will reverse, and buy the currency. When using this strategy, as long as you have predicted the reversal of the trend correctly, you will add money to your wallet.

The red and green indicators can also be used to make money, especially at the beginning of a trading day. the red indicators show that the closing price for the currency was more than the opening price, and the green indicator shows that the closing price was lower than the opening price. The green indicator shows that the price of the currency is likely to increase, especially during the first hours of the opening of the market. This is because the traders will anticipate an upward trend, and start selling, however, you should exchange the currency, and then have a closer observation that will help you exchange again quickly when there is a reverse in the trend.

Conclusion

Let's hope this was informative and able to provide you with all of the tools you need to achieve your goals whatever they may be.

This way, you will be able to visualize actual day trades without losing any money. Try and build your confidence this way and then move to an online trade simulator. Here, you will trade just like you would on a broker's platform. However, you will use virtual money.

It is only after you are thoroughly versed with day trading, including common terminology, day trading strategies, and so on that, you can now sign up with a broker and open a trading account. Day trading is very lucrative and can make you wealthy if applied well.

I want to take a moment before we part ways to celebrate you for investing the time in learning how to conduct day trading. Trading can be an intimidating topic, but as you may notice by now it is certainly not challenging to engage in once you know what you are doing. Although the stakes may seem higher because they involve cash money, the general consensus remains the same: as long as you continue to educate yourself on how to make this strategy work and you continue honing your skills, it will become easier.

There are many websites online that offer you the chance to try your hand at day trading on a simulator BEFORE you even start trading on a real market, and such websites are going to have to become an integral part of your study as you explore this field of trade.

Normal investors call day traders gamblers for a reason and that are because every day really is a gamble. Good day traders have been known to make over US$ 150,000 a year, but that does not mean they did not have their bad days where they lost a few thousand in the wrong security.

Remember, good discipline, and good money management is key to being a good day trader. Also, not allowing your emotions to run away with you when it is time to make a trade, or when you have heard some news is also imperative. Try as hard as possible to be logical and thorough when it comes to your trading practices, and with time even you could be making a 6 figure salary from the comfort of your home.

You absolutely have what it takes to be an excellent trader and to earn massive income through day trading stocks. Simply take your time getting started, educate yourself on each step as you go, build your confidence, and manage your mindset around your trades and you will be generating massive income in no time. The more you invest in building your confidence and your skill, the better you are going to become as a trader. Remember, you always want to strive for improvements even if you think you are already good enough as this is how you prevent yourself from becoming complacent. As long as you stay alert and focused, you will certainly become successful.